a mist shrouded path

poetry by
dusty grein

*cover design
and images*

© 2018, 2025
Flitterbow Productions

poetry and text

© 2018, 2025
Dusty Grein
all rights reserved

Second Edition, 2025

No part of this publication may be reproduced or transmitted in any form or by any means, electronic or mechanical, without prior written permission from the publisher and author.

ISBN-13: 978-1-949398-98-4

printed in the United States

Table of Contents

The Storm Within 1
Bridge of Memories 2
Hold My Hand In Yours 3
Greymoor Hall 4-5
Ode to a Soldier's Wife 6
Children 7
Dancing in the Wind 8
The Ocean Breaks 9
Thoughts from the Edge 10
The Missing Branch 11
Dwells A Troubled Mind 12
Within The Silvered Glass 13
Not Quite Sleeping 14-15
Upon Eagle Wings 16
Time to Fly 17
Freedom 18
Clouds 19
Morning Flight 20
A Mist Shrouded Path 21
In Her Emerald Eyes 22
Once Upon A Field Of Snow 23
Dressed in White 24-25
Left Behind 26
World of Wonder 27
Weeds 28
Just In Time 29
First Kiss 30
Sweet Recollections 31
Sweet Embrace 32
Exploration 33
A Dark Sun 34-35
White Wolf, Black Wolf 36
Do You See Me? 37
A Painted Smile 38

Angel Kisses	39
My Girl	40
Nowhere to Hide	41
A Dream Within A Dream	42
Behind My Dreams	43
Hot Air Balloons	44–45
Grandpa's Old Sedan	46
Loud Today	47
City of Light	48
Emergence	49
By Any Name	50
They're Gone	51
Veil of Gray	52
Mysterious Journey	53
Impatient Love	54–55
Before The Darkness	56
If Only	57
The Flame	58
Spectral Moon	59
Vows	60
A Mystery	61
The Portal	62–63
My Final Gift	64
Under the Summer Sun	65
Cold and Alone	66
Safe and Warm	67
Inheritance	68
She Lives	69
My Nightmare	70
Death Rides on Dark Wings	71
Within the Forest Deep	72–73
A Lonely Appendix	74
At The End	75
Dear God	76

Author's Foreword

There are places where the bright, clear world grows hazy and thin—where the air shifts, the light bends, and the familiar becomes a little strange around the edges. This book was born in places like that: moments when memories stirred like a shape wrapped in fog, and when a quiet invitation seemed to rise from the path itself, begging me to follow... even though I could not see where it led.

The mist is not simply weather—it is a threshold. It reveals the world in fragments, conceals mysteries with purpose, and reshapes whatever we believe we understand. It is patient, deliberate, and strangely alive.

The poems that follow were written while listening to what moves inside that shifting veil— echoes of old stories, glimpses of unspoken truths, and small revelations that feel borrowed from something much older than I am. Some poems came from grief, some from wonder, and some from those all-too-frequent moments when the world seemed to be speaking in symbols, rather than words.

I did not write these pages as explanations. I wrote them as lanterns—flickers of light placed beside a wandering trail, each one illuminating the path's edges. They often will show us where we have been, and occasionally they may light a few steps ahead... but they never reveal the whole journey.

The mist prefers it that way. It would rather guide than reveal; rather invite than declare.

As you walk through these poems, you may sense something moving just out of view—a presence, a question, a story half-remembered.

Some readers call it intuition. Some call it spirit. Some call it the part of us that listens and responds to the world behind the world.

Whatever you call it, it walks these pages with you.

The emotional terrain contained in these pages shifts like mist: storms rising and falling, memories blooming and fading, shadows sharpening then dissolving into light. Moments of ascension are followed by steep descents into the inner dark, and from those deep chambers within, unexpected light emerges again. This rhythm is no accident—it is the shape of every real journey... outer, inner, or sideways through time and space.

You may find stories here that resemble your own... or stories that feel like they belong to someone you once were... or stories that seem to come from places you've never been yet somehow remember.

Do not hurry them; the mist has its own pace. Let these poems be companions, but don't expect answers. Instead, allow them to widen the space around your thoughts, stir questions you had forgotten to ask, and offer quiet company on the lonely stretches of your life that feel furthest from clarity.

When you reach the final pages—those still, clear refuge spots near the edge of the unseen—I hope you feel the mist soften. It may not lift entirely, but I hope it will shift just enough to remind you that the world is deeper, and kinder, and more mysterious than it appears at first glance.

Thank you for stepping into the unknown with me. May the path, however obscured, lead you toward something worth discovering.

— Dusty Grein, 2025

The Storm Within

Across the sky, a cannonade;
black-bellied clouds give chase
as lightning joins the dark parade,
and chill winds howl and race.
I bundle up against the storm
to ride it out until the morn.
    I bundle up,
    I bundle up,
yet in my soul, I can't get warm.

Staccato rain begins to drum,
the world now dressed in gray
as icy water sheets and runs
and washes hope away.
My silent tears fall to the floor
as darkness has its way once more.
    My silent tears,
    my silent tears
flow like the rain, from eyes grown

I close my eyes and rest my brow
upon the window pane
and listen to the wretched sound
of unrelenting rain.
I say your name and in reply
no answer comes but stormy skies.
    I say your name
    I say your name,
then slowly hang my head and cry.

Bridge of Memories

A bridge built of memories

spans the gap between future and past.
Although life may speed by us too fast,

from every experience, knowledge we gain.
Far too many moments for us to retain
each second of happiness, boredom and pain;
the best and the worst are the ones that remain.

In the end, what we've actually amassed
on this foundation, crafted to last,

a bridge built of memories.

Hold my hand in yours; we'll make it through.
If life becomes too hard to comprehend,
for no one understands me like you do.

Along life's lonely road, I'll walk with you.
When times are hard, please know you have a friend.
Hold my hand in yours; we'll make it through.

I'm here for you. You give me your strength too;
my courage is no longer just pretend,
for no one understands me like you do.

My friend, I'll cheer you up when you are blue,
A smile, my heart to yours will always send.
Hold my hand in yours; we'll make it through.

If I am down, you make me feel brand new
You know the way, my broken heart to mend,
for no one understands me like you do.

Though often life presents a horrid view,
Together we can face the bitter end.
Hold my hand in yours; we'll make it through,
for no one understands me like you do.

Hold My Hand in Yours

Dust lies thick in empty hallways; as the light begins to fade
chill wind swirls down ancient chimneys, cold and dry as brittle bone.
The old mansion lies uneasy, knowing dues must still be paid.
Even though there is no movement in its rooms it's not alone,
    for the restless souls who died here have been trapped and still remain
    and the house, once filled with laughter, has grown evil and insane;
    now no happiness is found here—only anguish, fear, and pain.
        In the attic is a nursery, used by little ones no more,
        where abandoned in one corner, sits a broken china doll;
        while the bowels of the building hold a pit in earthen floor.
        From this well without a bottom,
            comes the curse of Greymoor Hall.

In the days before the curse fell, when the house was newly made—
standing strong against the weather, its foundation solid stone—
there was light and there was laughter, and here children gaily played.
Often music could be heard, as peaceful moonlight sweetly shone,
    every season was spent happy in the sun, and snow, and rain
    but the house, once filled with love, has now completely gone insane,
    for its memories of those years, although skewed, are yet retained.
        It remembers distant yesterdays, bright waves upon a shore,
        but an evil and dark undertow has clouded its recall.
        The despair of hope abandoned is a throaty distant roar
        from the well without a bottom,
            in the heart of Greymoor Hall.

In those days beautiful Anna was a sweet and buxom maid,
but her love for young Paul Greymoor meant the seeds of death were sown,
for she gave to him her flower—in the basement dirt they laid.
There, the final drop of virgin blood was spilled with breathy moans,
    and her sacrifice of innocence, into the well did drain.
    Soon the house was filled with screaming and the sound drove it insane,
    as the ductwork rang with echoes and the walls with ichor stained.
        Bittersweet, her loss of purity had opened up a door;
        in the depths of Hell a demon turned its head toward her blood's call
        on its face it wore an evil grin, as if it knew the score.
        From the well without a bottom,
            it climbed into Greymoor Hall.

Greymoor Hall

These young lovers were the first two upon whom the demon preyed,
and their ravaged bodies, still alive, into the pit were thrown
ere the monster threw its head back, laughing vile cannonades,
and the solid walls around it seemed to buckle and to groan.
   Darkness gushed forth from the well, like blood from out an open vein;
   as the house filled up with evil, all its dreams became insane
   and the stench of deadly decay simply could not be contained.
      Through the other living residents' weak flesh the demon tore.
      With the ending of their lives, the final barrier did fall,
      these environs were inhabited by living souls no more
      and the well without a bottom
         held full sway at Greymoor Hall.

Near a century has passed now since that unholy parade
and the grounds around the building lie weed-choked and overgrown.
Faded wallpaper sags, peeling; window coverings are frayed,
and once lustrous marble fixtures now lie shattered and flyblown.
   In the ballroom jet black spiders and white maggots darkly reign,
   while the basement, full of shadows, echoes laughter quite insane
   and this sound which can't be heard, is one that science can't explain.
      Faintly glowing in the moonlight are green putrid fungus spores
      which reflect upon the insects who 'cross ancient remains crawl
      near the blood red evil light source which shines forth, a blighted sore
      from the well without a bottom,
         far below old Greymoor Hall.

It is said the ghosts of Anna and Paul Greymoor, though insane
   are still haunting rooms and hallways now grown wicked to the core,
   and the demon they set free that day still lives within the walls;
   Any humans who set foot inside, will find out what's in store,
   and the well without a bottom
      will be fed in Greymoor Hall.

Ode to a Soldier's Wife

I can see your tears are streaming, in the lamp light they are gleaming.
How I wish that I were dreaming and that duty hadn't called.
Through the wretched bars we're kissing as the steam train begins hissing,
and of all the things worth missing I shall miss you most of all.
Although I am on a mission, moonlight on us both will glisten.
In the night, just sit and listen; love I'll send straight to your hall
in the night bird's lonely call.

Please have faith and keep on praying in God's grace we'll both be staying.
All the soldiers here are saying that the end of war is near.
Though in truth, it would be lying if I said I weren't crying,
in my heart I shall be trying not to give in to my fear.
Your sweet smile I'll keep adoring in my mind. Though it be pouring,
know my spirit will be soaring far above my mortal tears
'til your voice, again I hear.

As I turn, already yearning, there's a truth that I am learning.
Loneliness commences burning deep within my broken heart.
Now the captain's voice is urging and the engine begins surging.
Frosty air and steam are merging as my eyes rapidly dart
toward the gate where she is clinging. The conductor's bell is ringing
and the soldiers take up singing. Now the train slowly departs
as my soul is torn apart.

In my empty bedroom, trying not to give in to my sighing,
hearing ought but my clock's ticking in the evening's waning glow.
Candlelight for sunlight traded, long deep shadows have invaded;
day's bright colors now are faded as my thoughts begin to flow;
images my mind is picking up from days of long ago,
watching as my children grow.

Mirth and sorrow, both are lying in the dust of recall, vying
for the right to seal the bargain and the final punch to throw.
From the day of birth we're fated to be both adored and hated;
scales of life are tipped and weighted, good and evil, to and fro.
We must strip away the jargon and get to the truth below;
relearn what the children know.

When the tears are all done drying; after laughter, after crying,
on the final day of judging, which direction will we go?
Earthly deeds will then be rated, cause and effect finally mated
and the truth no longer shaded by false pride and our ego.
Family ties ensure us Heaven; one last gift they do bestow—
all the love our children show.

Children

Dancing in the Wind

Buffeted by winds of change, I gaze in wonder at the fractal patterns of shifting shadows, as life swirls around me. Swaying to the rhythms of nature, every experience shapes my growth, adding to my resolve. I must not fight these changes, but find instead a way for them to make me stronger.

dancing in the wind
standing brave before the storm
face turned to the sky
weakness quickly stripped away
'bend don't break' grants survival

Twilight, and the ocean breaks
my bleeding heart once more.
Relentlessly the salty waves
crash hard, and rocks are worn.
I cry in rage and shake my fist.
Screaming aloud my bitter list,
I cry in rage!
I cry in rage,
the sea answers with surf and mist.

Twilight, and the ocean breaks
upon the rock-strewn shore;
now comes the dawn. My pain's awake
and misery's reborn.
Your tender heart and gentle kiss
are gone now, and I I truly miss
your tender heart
your tender heart
and all our special midnight trysts.

Twilight, and the ocean breaks
in never-ending score
of push and pull. My anger fades
as night gives way to morn.
Within my soul you still exist;
it helps me to remember this
within my soul.
Within my soul,
your heart and mine, forever twist.

The Ocean Breaks

Thoughts from the Edge

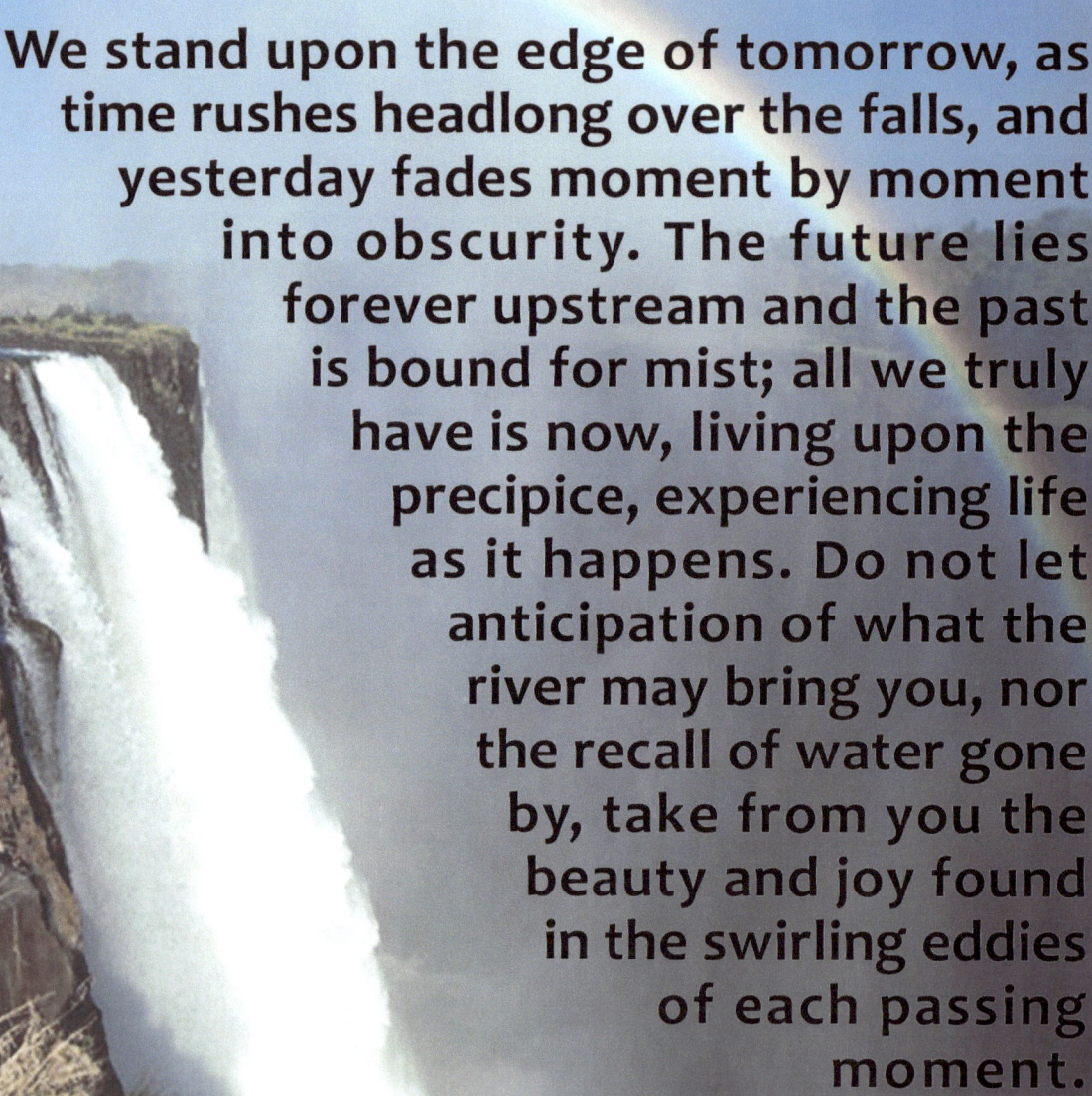

We stand upon the edge of tomorrow, as time rushes headlong over the falls, and yesterday fades moment by moment into obscurity. The future lies forever upstream and the past is bound for mist; all we truly have is now, living upon the precipice, experiencing life as it happens. Do not let anticipation of what the river may bring you, nor the recall of water gone by, take from you the beauty and joy found in the swirling eddies of each passing moment.

upon time's river
memories fade into haze
leaving only now

The Missing Branch

Family trees may bear much fruit, yet some branches never get to grow. Occasionally we must face the mortality of youth, and our loss scars the bark and molds the tree. We cherish every leaf and find the blooms are still as sweet, though now watered with our eyes.

empty heart still beats
bare branches cry out in vain
silent teardrops fall

In bitter darkness dwells a troubled mind;
while searching for a true love to adore,
deep loneliness is all that it can find.

Sweet fantasies play brief and then rewind
deep midnight dreams upon a rocky shore
in bitter darkness dwells a troubled mind.

With darkling madness never far behind--
like rotten fruit, bleeds ebon at its core--
deep loneliness is all that it can find.

Pain floats like foam upon the churning brine
emotions on a sea without support,
in bitter darkness dwells a troubled mind.

Anger becomes magnetically aligned
with memories, strewn vast upon the floor;
deep loneliness is all that it can find.

Dwells A Troubled Mind

Within the Silvered Glass

Within the silvered glass I spy
the mask I wear, my perfect lie.
This happy face, it is not me;
I show them what they want to see
while deep inside I slowly die.

I cannot let them see me cry,
so I just smile and wave goodbye
then check for signs of pain, set free
within the silvered glass.

With broken wings I'll never fly;
I turn away and softly sigh.
My world consists of tragedy –
a scream that echoes silently.
The fools can't see, it is not I,
within the silvered glass.

As I sit here not quite sleeping,
in the comfort of my chair,
while the fire's warmth is keeping
wintry drafts out of the air,
   both my eyes are slowly blinking
   and their surface starts to glaze;
   Slowly I feel my chin sinking,
   here before the crackling blaze.

   Lo, the moonlight's stealthy creeping
   'cross the window's icy stare
   as I sit here, not quite sleeping
   in the comfort of my chair.
      In my mind's eye daydreams dawning
      as the room begins to blur.
      Gritty eyes and languid yawning,
      my surrender seems assured.

Not Quite Sleeping

Bands of flick'ring firelight throwing
spectral shadows on the wall,
heavy drowsiness keeps growing,
though I'm trying not to fall.
   *As I sit here, not quite sleeping
    in the comfort of my chair,*
   swirled thoughts like hounds are leaping,
   chasing some elusive hare.

   Neither wide awake nor snoozing,
   silent lullabies float by
   consciousness I'm slowly losing;
   breathing stretches into sighs.
      Quiet minutes by me sweeping,
      and in truth, I just don't care
      *as I sit here, not quite sleeping
      in the comfort of my chair.*

Upon Eagle Wings

    Under a crystal dome of deepest blue
     Perfection balanced on an unseen breeze
      Observing as his realm rolls into view
       Nature's majestic raptor floats with ease

        Ever aware of movements far below
         Across the sky he sails, a stringless kite
          Graceful and free to dip and glide and soar,
           Limits unknown, traversing highest heights
            Ethereal as dreams now taken flight.

             With lightning speed, swift death to prey he brings
              Intensity within his star-burst eyes.
               No malice does he carry on the wing
                Gaze up and you will find with no suprise
                 Sun-drenched, he carries beauty as he flies.

Please smile when you think of me,
and all the things we've done.
Look past the pain, I think you'll see
Your journey's just begun.
My path is clear and leads away
From yours right now, but it's okay
    My path is clear
    My path is clear;
the setting sun will light my way.

The empty bed I left behind,
I hope you understand.
Please don't think me too unkind.
This wasn't what I planned.
I found a song I had to start;
now I must sing, though we're apart.
    I found a song,
    I found a song,
and now my feet follow my heart.

Of days and nights spent in your arms,
sweet memories survive.
I fondly recall all your charms
and love is still alive.
I spread my wings, lessons to learn.
My chin held high without concern
    I spread my wings,
    I spread my wings;
who knows, one day I may return.

Time to Fly

Adrift upon a cold and stormy sea
The waves tossed me about quite cruelly
Until I learned how to survive the ride
No longer will life's storms discourage me

I used to be a victim of the tide,
of circumstance, of selfishness, of pride;
quite often I would hide my face and cry
Ashamed of who I was down deep inside.

One darkened day, a prayer I thought I'd try;
a voice said clearly, "Stand and say goodbye
to fear and hate and anger; you should know
that you were born with wings, so learn to fly."

The tide still surges and the wind still blows,
but now I stand defiantly and throw
my head back and proclaim aloud, "I'm free!"
as fearlessly I face the vast unknown.

Freedom

Clouds

Clouds drift across the peaceful azure sky.
As I sit quietly under this tree,
I think of life's big questions and then sigh.
I wonder if someday I'll truly see.

As I sit quietly under this tree,
the sun is shining warm upon my face.
I wonder if someday I'll truly see
the beauty hidden deep inside this place .

The sun is shining warm upon my face.
I stretch out, gladly soaking up the light,
the beauty hidden deep inside this place,
as arms of golden warmth embrace me tight.

I stretch out, gladly soaking up the light.
I think of life's big questions and then sigh;
as arms of golden warmth embrace me tight,
clouds drift across the peaceful azure sky.

Morning Flight

It was a dark and stormy night;
now dawn has birthed another day.
I sense the morning's growing light,
then grabbing air… up, up, away…
it's time to spread my wings in flight!
The world awaits, I will not stay;
all caution to the wind I've thrown.
I soar the heights, free and alone.

Nothing has ever felt so right!
Upon the breeze I dip and play.
Above the clouds, the sky is bright
while far below, still somewhat gray,
the rainfall stops. Now comes the sight
of sunshine breaking nighttime's sway.
As thunder mumbles one last groan,
the land once more, by daytime owned.

Flapping my wings with all my might,
the fields and streams below me lay.
I drift and float, a stringless kite
to ride the currents come what may.
Freedom hard won, I hold it tight
and wait out nighttime storms. You say
for doubt and fear I must atone,
yet with the dawn I will have flown.

A Mist Shrouded Path

Alone did I roam down a mist shrouded path,
where icy fog swallowed the faintest of sounds,
a victim of fear, and cruel heaven's wrath.

The pain in my heart I had carefully bound;
my feet led me deeper, far into the gray,
as if some enlightenment, there could be found.

Faint spectral trees watched as I knelt down to pray-
in answer, there came to me naught but deep gloom.
What small faith I'd had, I'd cast blindly away.

After losing them both, before new life could bloom;
grief flooded my soul with its poisonous bath
and fog-wrapped, the silence foreshadowed my doom.

Avoiding the pain that was all my heart hath,
alone did I roam down a mist shrouded path.

In Her Emerald Eyes

In her emerald eyes,
promise and surprise
shine bright,
followed by her sighs.
I will compromise
tonight,
fall for all her lies,
though I know it unwise.

Too late to revise
I now recognize
my plight.
Slow to realize,
my soul weakly tries
to fight;
dark hopes soon arise
in her emerald eyes.

Pain, like teardrops, dries
as sweet passion's cries
take flight.
Resistance soon dies,
inhibition flies
despite
moans, which now comprise
promise and surprise.

None may criticize--
I won't exercise
the right.
Lips tremble, flexed thighs
sweat, and breathy sighs
soon light
promise and surprise
in her emerald eyes.

Once Upon a Field of Snow

Once upon a field of snow
a babe was put to breast;
his mother's sparkling eyes aglow
with love, she did impress
his love for her so deep and true
that every ounce of his soul knew
    his love for her.
    His love for her
waxed stronger daily as he grew

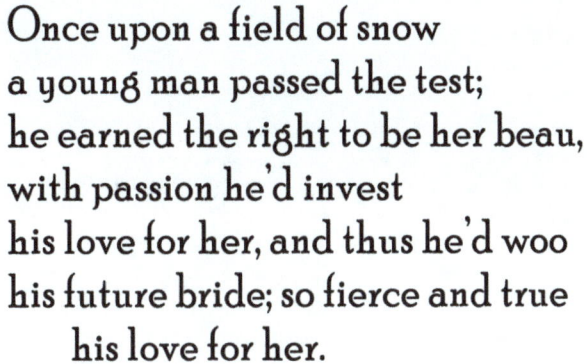

    Once upon a field of snow
    a young man passed the test;
    he earned the right to be her beau,
    with passion he'd invest
    his love for her, and thus he'd woo
    his future bride; so fierce and true
        his love for her.
        His love for her
    gave his heart wings, with which they flew.

        Once upon a field of snow
        a heart was laid to rest;
        his soul mate, he had watched her go,
        his tear-filled eyes confessed
        his love for her, so strong and true.
        His future, shaded gray and blue
            his love for her.
            His love for her
        would somehow help him see it through.

Soft by torchlight I roam, seeking
thru the dark'ning woods of weeping
willows, her lithe figure keeping
just beyond the edge of sight.

By the flick'ring flame the shadows
dance like felons 'pon the gallows,
still the mystery woman follows
her path by mere lantern's light.

Subtle glimpses of her fleeting
form I chase into the night,
this mystery maiden
dressed in white.

Dressed in

Suddenly I find her, standing
in the moonlight, eyes demanding
my surrender. She's commanding
me to proceed without fright.

There, beneath raven hair flowing,
I can see her skin is glowing;
and my fear, which should be growing
deep inside, has taken flight.

Pale blue firelight now dancing
in her hands; a spectral sight,
supernatural beauty
dressed in white.

Forward my feet slowly moving
toward this creature, as if proving
heavy debts my soul's accruing,
and I lose my will to fight.

With intent I step up closer,
craving, needing just to know her;
days of free will are quite over,
as I'm wrapped in chains of light.

Eldritch witch-fire soon engulfs me,
eating my soul, burning bright
while she watches
dressed in white.

Closer, she leans in to kiss me.
As our lips meet, I grow dizzy
then she smiles, whispers softly,
"Love, come closer, hold me tight."

White

In my embrace she is clinging,
as the angels commence singing
I ignore the painful stinging,
when my neck she gives a bite.

With a grin she sends me hither,
seeking victims in the night -
my new mistress
dressed in white.

Left Behind

Born in beauty and in light - pure, serene
raised with dreams all taking flight
sweet by day, mystery by night.

Too soon you had to leave me - left behind,
in my mind, it seems I'll be
alone for eternity.

Slow now, the gentle beating - my sad heart,
e'er apart, still repeating;
in silent pain retreating.

All the angels start singing - soft as birds,
joyous words, while taking wing,
echo "love is everything."

World Of Wonder

Alone, I often confer
and walk with Mother Nature,
awe reflected on my face;
the world, a place of wonder.

Angel kisses from on high,
borne on wings of butterflies,
these are proof empirical,
small miracles, flying by.

If dark clouds I see ahead,
I won't give in to hatred
when showers fall from above,
I'll let love shine forth instead.

Beauty oft makes my heart sing,
or finds tears of joy starting
in my eyes, as dew at dawn
shines upon the grass of Spring.

Weeds

Like weeds among the flowers in my yard,
you took root in my soul and blocked the sun;
I wish my heart was barren, dry and hard.

There was a time when loving you was fun,
but now it's only leeches at the lake;
the damage done inside can't be undone.

It seems the tenderness we shared was fake,
like pink flamingos at my Grandma's house
or toothpaste icing on a birthday cake.

The spark of passion in my core's been doused,
and wisdom seems a lousy end reward
for watching as you leave, once-trusted spouse.

You proved my dreams were but a house of cards,
like weeds among the flowers in my yard.

Just in Time

Our fate has brought us here in time to meet.
Two travelers upon a lonely trail,
the raging river churning past our feet.

The misty air replaces summer's heat
while turning both our faces slightly pale;
our fate has brought us here in time to meet.

Her eyes reflecting mine are kind and sweet;
she turns away to hide from me her tale,
the raging river churning past our feet.

Some other time and place, another street...
But no! Such thoughts will pave the way to fail,
and fate has brought us here in time to meet!

Together now, with no chance to retreat.
We form a team, our destiny to sail
the raging river churning past our feet

Her tear streaked face makes my soul feel complete
as hand-in-hand we climb over the rail.
Our fate has brought us here in time to meet
the raging river churning past our feet.

First Kiss

I floated home on clouds the day we met;
that first great kiss changed everything and more.
My life was full of "Haven't done that yet,"
(I'd never tasted someone's tongue before).

That first great kiss changed everything and more;
you taught me what it was to fall in love.
I'd never tasted someone's tongue before,
but kissing, for you, just wasn't enough.

You taught me what it was to fall in love.
My virgin hands were unsure what to do,
but kissing, for you, just wasn't enough.
You made me want to learn the rest from you.

My virgin hands were unsure what to do –
my life was full of "Haven't done that yet."
You made me want to learn the rest from you;
I floated home on clouds the day we met.

Tea time, just my mom and me
memories so sweet and dear,
knowing I was her first choice;
still her voice is crystal clear.

Some of my favorite hours.
fresh cut flowers in a vase,
aroma drifting after,
her bright laughter giving chase.

Drinks poured from a silver pot,
piping hot, a cup of tea;
better than all the others
my mother's best, just for me.

Subtle taste of chamomile
Love revealed in Earl Grey
My sweet tooth she would appease
"Two lumps please," I'd smile and say.

Sweet drinks still can take me back
Down the track toward yesterday
It's been years we've been apart—
In my heart, she'll always stay

Sweet Recollections

Love's Sweet Embrace

In love's sweet embrace I fly, bereft of wings.
At your touch, my feet lose contact with the ground;
my spirit, thus freed from harsh gravity, sings.

I'm dancing on air, gaily spinning around -
a kiss from your gentle lips pauses the world,
as thunderous echoes vibrate without sound.

My heart's tender petals begin to unfurl;
each beat of my pulse a staccato drum beat.
The seed of pain deep within, becomes a pearl.

Reflected in your eyes, my joy is complete.
Your sweet smile, to my face, true happiness brings;
fans passion's raw embers to glorious heat.

Concerns drift away, of all worldly things;
in love's sweet embrace, I fly bereft of wings.

Journeys lead us foot by foot - foul or fair,
whether bare or clad in boot,
under limb and over root.

Chins held high or tucked in fear - we must choose,
win or lose; trips far and near
lead us all to there, from here.

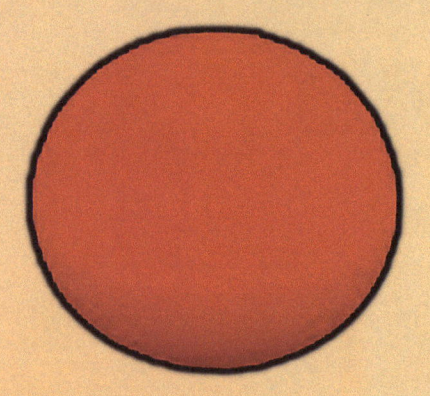

Free from worry she is spinning,
dancing, twirling, brightly grinning,
as her final day's beginning,
'neath the dark sun,
ruby red.

Caring not about the glances
of her neighbors as she dances
on this final day of chances,
'neath the dark sun,
ruby red.

In the sky the birds are wheeling.
She finds joy to be appealing
for this final day of feeling
'neath the dark sun,
ruby red,

dying dark sun
overhead.

Scientific fears abiding,
on an error hopes were riding;
at the end, there was no hiding
from the dark sun
flying high.

First warnings were taken lightly;
now, while holding loved ones tightly
Near the end, the light bursts brightly
from the dark sun
flying high.

Most have no real way of learning,
'til deep red, the clouds are turning;
in the end the air starts burning
from the dark sun
flying high,

dying dark sun
in the sky.

All their great works torn asunder,
instantly, in silent thunder.
No one left to sit and wonder
where the dark sun
used to be.

An expanding glowing bubble
rapidly it's size had doubled;
nothing left to cause more trouble
where the dark sun
used to be.

Super-nova quickly growing
eating planets without slowing;
empty space is what's left, showing
where the dark sun
used to be,

dark sun once,
now memory.

White Wolf, Black Wolf

Inside you lives a wolf of white ~~
of patience, peace and love.
He is forgiveness, hope and light;
a blessing from above.
This wolf of white the world will see
through all the good he brings to thee.
    This wolf of white,
      this wolf of white,
his gifts will set your spirit free.

    A wolf of black, as dark as night
    lives next to him inside.
    He's hatred, rage, cruelty, fright,
    intolerance and pride.
    This wolf of black the world will see
    through evil actions, cruel deeds.
      This wolf of black,
        this wolf of black,
    his teeth will make your spirit bleed.

      Within your soul, the two wolves fight
      to see which one will give
      directions and will win the right
      to show you how to live.
      Which one will win the fight? We need
      to pay attention; pay close heed!
        Which one will win?
        Which one will win
      depends upon which one we feed.

Do You See Me?

*Sitting here, I'm hurting, feeling
fear, despair, regret, and need.
My life, no one finds appealing,
no one ever pays much heed.
I can understand the worry...
pity hurts, so don't come near;
act like you are in a hurry.
Do you even see me here?*

*Sober, I'm not stumbling, reeling,
look away while my heart bleeds;
human contact could bring healing.
Smiling — such a simple deed,
if our eyes meet, you get weepy,
sorrow battling with your fear...
maybe you just find me creepy.
Do you even see me here?*

*On your cell phone, wheeling, dealing,
pretend you don't hear my plea.
Maybe my fate you are sealing
walking past me, down the street.
I hide behind my grim eyes, only
wanting not to shed these tears;
wishing my life weren't so lonely.
Do you even see me here?*

*Watching you, I sit silently,
seeing things, so crystal clear;
hatred hurts me less than pity...
do you even see me here?*

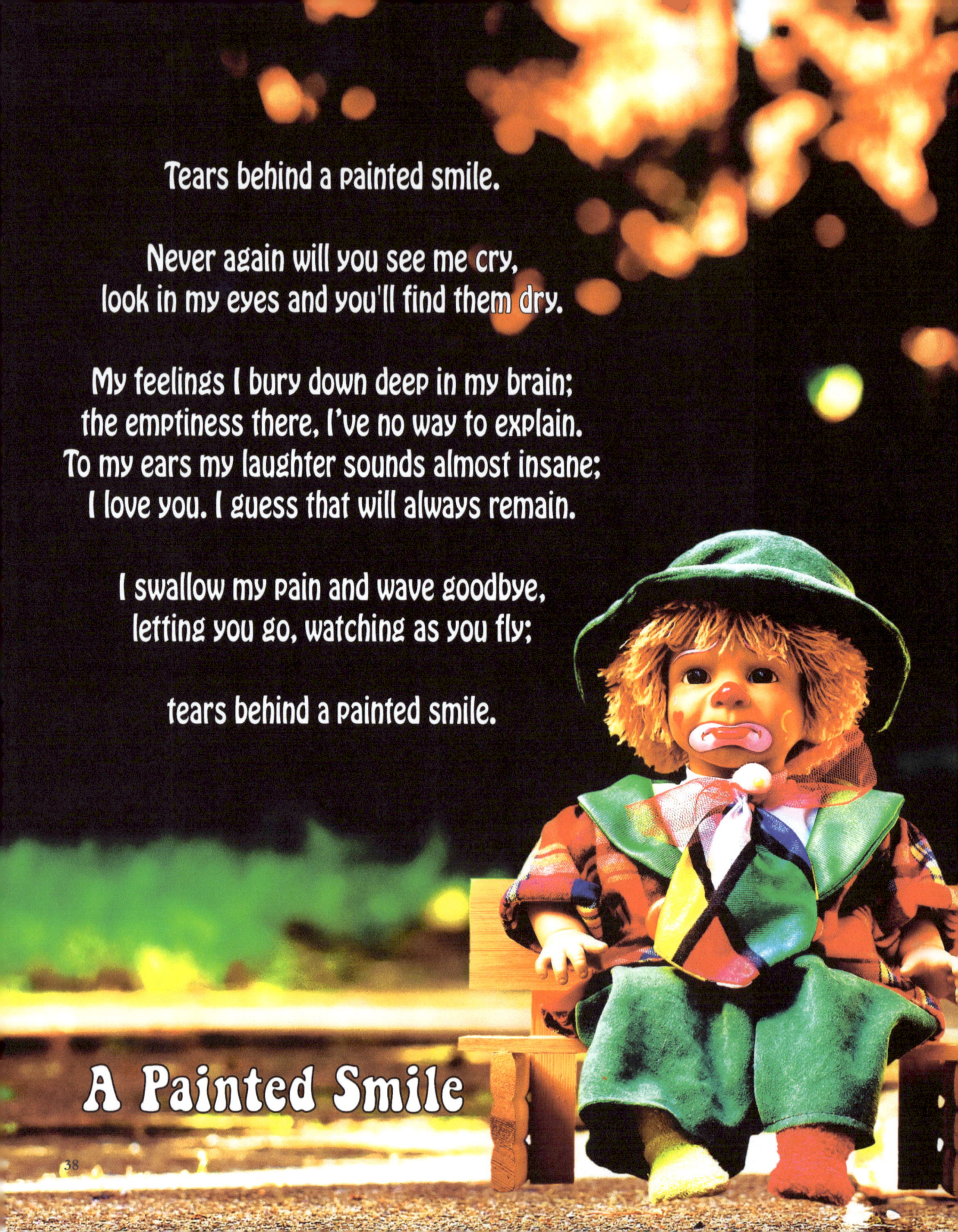

Tears behind a painted smile.

Never again will you see me cry,
look in my eyes and you'll find them dry.

My feelings I bury down deep in my brain;
the emptiness there, I've no way to explain.
To my ears my laughter sounds almost insane;
I love you. I guess that will always remain.

I swallow my pain and wave goodbye,
letting you go, watching as you fly;

tears behind a painted smile.

A Painted Smile

The blessed see the world with more than eyes,
for hearts can see much more of nature's truth,
like angel kisses from a butterfly...
these things I took for granted in my youth.

Our hearts can see much more of nature's truth
sweet messages gifted on fragile wings
were things I took for granted in my youth
and in the quiet moments, heaven sings!

Sweet messages like gifts on fragile wings
are signs bestowed from loved ones up above,
and in the quiet moments, heaven sings
in thundering silence, echoing our love.

For signs bestowed from loved ones up above,
these angel kisses brought by butterflies
will, in their thundering silence, echo love;
the blessed see the world with more than eyes.

Angel Kisses

Any dreams she wants to plan - they're in reach
I will teach her that she can;
she's as tough as any man.

She must play, to win or lose - stand or fall
she will always have to choose
from her tools, which she will use.

She may dress in silk and lace - yet she knows
that there's so much more to grace
than smiles on her pretty face.

All grown up, she'll hit the street - head to head
she'll be ready to compete;
and I'll know my job's complete.

My Girl

It's midnight, and the whispers begin,
softly echoing plans to do harm
from the demons inside of my skin.

I'm unable to sound the alarm
when the demons all try to escape,
softly echoing plans to do harm.

Horrid visions of murder and rape,
as the doors in my mind open wide
and the demons all try to escape.

Far too many to hold them inside,
so at last I give in to their screams
and the doors in my mind open wide.

In black voices they share darker dreams;
with a smile and a gleam in my eye
once again I give in to their screams.

The fell beasts in my mind I let fly
as I smile with a gleam in my eye...
for at midnight the whispers begin
from the demons inside of my skin.

NOWHERE TO HIDE

A Dream Within A Dream

As clouds break over fallen temple walls,
pale moonlight steps among the misty moors.
Soft gentle breezes whisper silent calls
    as clouds break over fallen temple walls;
the magic realms of old open their halls,
sweet mystery like nectar slowly pours.
    As clouds break over fallen temple walls,
pale moonlight steps among the misty moors.

    Pale moonlight steps among the misty moors.
    White hooves softly approach the silent lake,
    ephemeral, translucence on the shore.
        Pale moonlight steps among the misty moors;
    a dream within a dream from days of yore
    which human hearts would never dare to wake.
        Pale moonlight steps among the misty moors;
    white hooves softly approach the silent lake.

    White hooves softly approach the silent lake
    as clouds break over fallen temple walls.
    A flash of horn revealed by gentle shake,
        white hooves softly approach the silent lake.
    Dark Nox herself, this spell is loathe to break,
    for wondrousness, beside this vision palls;
        white hooves softly approach the silent lake
    as clouds break over fallen temple walls.

In vistas dark behind my dreams
I am at ease
with fantasies;
here, truth is never what it seems.
On currents strong,
I drift along
secure within sweet sleep's embrace,
and find at night
a brief respite
from cares, which waking, I must face.

Behind My Dreams

We climb into the early morning sky.
As sunlight paints away the grays of night
the day's rebirth we witness with a sigh.
  We climb into the early morning sky
  and dawn breaks over eastern mountains high,
  exploding in symphonic colored light.
    We climb into the early morning sky
    as sunlight paints away the grays of night.

    As sunlight paints away the grays of night
    the world below begins to come awake;
    adrift above, I'm humbled by the sight.
      As sunlight paints away the grays of night
      the dawn reflects the hope of future bright,
      a chance to start anew, despite mistakes.
        As sunlight paints away the grays of night,
        the world below begins to come awake.

Hot Air Balloons
(Welcoming the Dawn)

The world below begins to come awake
while sunshine once more banishes the dark.
Who knows what difference today might make?
   The world below begins to come awake
   and dawn's sweet light, reflected on the lake
   shows all the world that night has left no mark.
     The world below begins to come awake,
     while sunshine once more banishes the dark

     While sunshine once more banishes the dark,
     we climb into the early morning sky--
     the home of both the eagle and the lark.
       While sunshine once more banishes the dark,
       the dawn ignites the world with heaven's spark
       and beauty that oft makes the strong man cry.
         While sunshine once more banishes the dark,
         we climb into the early morning sky.

Grandpa's Old Sedan

Frost clinging to the trees and grass,
we wandered 'cross the farm,
and happened on the rusted shell
   of Grandpa's old sedan.

A memory of days long past,
one time could never harm,
now decades past the new-car smell
   of Grandpa's old sedan.

There was a time it went quite fast,
this relic, past the barn;
each dent and scratch, a story tells,
   of Grandpa's old sedan.

As his first love, its role was cast.
before his call-to-arms,
life's imprint in each metal cell
   of Grandpa's old sedan.

It might have been the price of gas,
which far outpaced its charm,
that sounded out the last death knell
   of Grandpa's old sedan.

A remnant that was built to last,
no seat belts or alarms,
yet magic lives within the spell
   of Grandpa's old sedan.

Loud Today

The voices in my head are loud today,
I plug my ears, but still I hear them talk
Oh please, oh please just make them go away!

I thought that maybe I could take a walk
That they would quiet down and let me think
I plug my ears, but still I hear them talk

I'm trying not to let my spirit sink,
These voices drowning out my fervent plea
That they would quiet down and let me think

I hear them use my mouth. That wasn't me!
Oh please help me ignore their foul demands
These voices drowning out my fervent plea

I hang my head, then fiercely wring my hands
As they tell me to do such evil things
Oh please help me ignore their foul demands

Pure misery their constant echoes bring,
As they tell me to do such evil things
The voices in my head are loud today,
Oh please, oh please just make them go away!

City of Light

I dreamed of a city of light,
a beacon of hope glowing white
where beauty and art
are ever a part
of its heart, shining bright.

A glorious city of light
outshining the moon in its flight,
as sweet as a dove
which flying above,
sings of love's magic sight.

My soul is a city of light
where darkness is losing the fight—
for love left its mark,
igniting a spark
in the dark of the night.

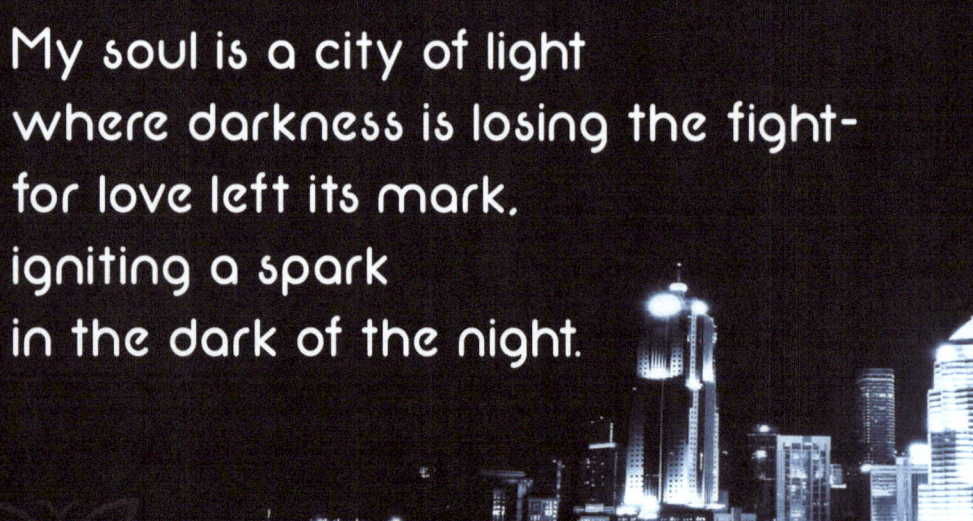

Within my shell, I held inside
a secret glow;
allowed to grow,
until it was too large to hide.
I let no tears
betray my fears,
as quietly I stayed on task;
until at last
the die was cast,
and breaking free, I shed the mask.

Emergence

By Any Name

Amorphophallus Titanum
(Corpse Flower)

Oh, how I wish I were a rose,
a flower with aroma sweet,
While I offend the human nose,
because I smell like rotting meat!

A flower with aroma sweet
is not the way my story goes;
instead I'm huge with body heat!
Oh, how I wish I were a rose.

While I offend the human nose,
(as if to make my shame complete)
this lovely rose beside me grows,
a flower with aroma sweet.

Because I smell like rotting meat,
Corpse Flower is my name, not rose.
For roses, sweet perfumes excrete,
while I offend the human nose.

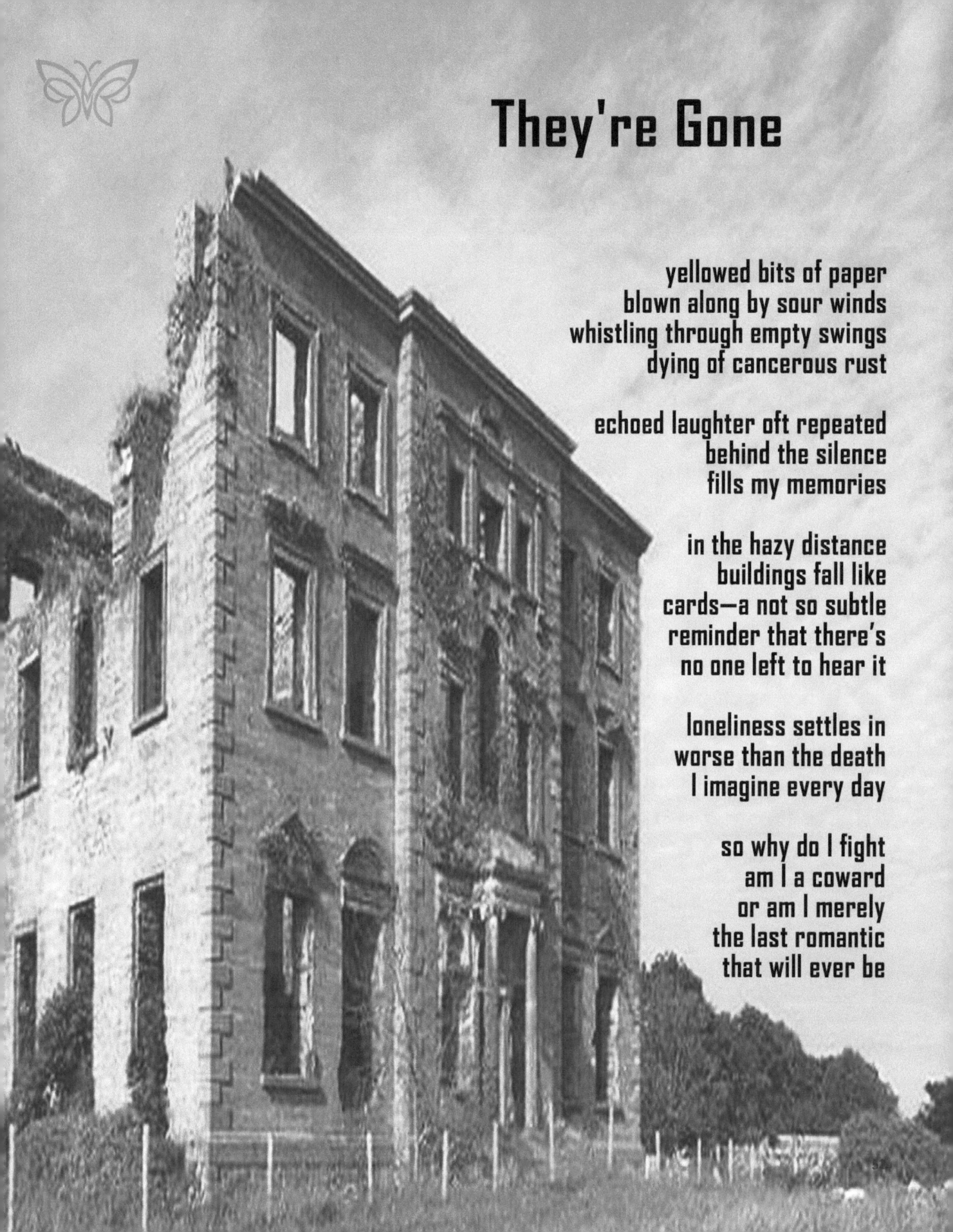

They're Gone

yellowed bits of paper
blown along by sour winds
whistling through empty swings
dying of cancerous rust

echoed laughter oft repeated
behind the silence
fills my memories

in the hazy distance
buildings fall like
cards—a not so subtle
reminder that there's
no one left to hear it

loneliness settles in
worse than the death
I imagine every day

so why do I fight
am I a coward
or am I merely
the last romantic
that will ever be

Veil of Gray

With its veil of gray,
fog yet holds full sway.
Delight
as dawn leads the way
in mystic display;
hold tight
while the misty day
keeps color at bay.

O'er hill and highway,
ground fog softly strays
and slight
subtle shades portray
monochrome arrays;
pale white
hidden secrets play
in its veil of gray.

Soon the sunshine may
burn the mists away
and bright
noon's hues will betray
golden fields of hay.
Sunlight
in the future lays;
fog yet holds full sway.

Though the clouds have frayed,
daylight is delayed.
Dark night
spends time here today;
shadows strong will stay
in sight.
Fog yet holds full sway
with its veil of gray.

Mysterious Journey

Beginnings shrouded in the mists of time,
this lifelong ride begins with our first breath.
Through vales we dip, and up steep hills we climb,
our path leads ever onward unto death.

We plot our course in darkness through the night;
the tracks of time lead us we know not where,
the future stretches out beyond the light --
we rush headlong and trust it will be there.

To plan ahead or leave it all to fate...
these are the options we must choose between.
The truth of revelation oft is late.
While looking back we see just where we've been,

No one can know the future that awaits.
Within the dark lie mysteries unseen.

impatient love

the empty spot upon my rumpled bed
matches the aching place within my heart.
my pillow bears the imprint of your head;
I hate this dreadful time that we're apart.

I'm sitting here alone and incomplete
while dreaming of your fingers in my hair;
the taste of your lips on mine remains sweet.
your scent lingers upon the morning air.

my fingers trace the outlines of your touch;
inside my core a fiery heat begins.
pulse racing, I can feel my face go flush,
remembering your breath upon my skin.

this unquenched passion now will slowly burn,
until we reach the hour of your return.

I wait upon the hour of your return,
so while you're gone, I let my mind run free.
the tender parts of me I'll help you learn,
and secret things I'll let you do to me.

I picture us, entwined within these sheets;
a smile upon my lips begins to show.
within my breast, my heart rapidly beats
and moisture deep inside me starts to grow.

I settle in this soft nest of satin
and let my fingers travel where they will.
they quickly find a spot of hungry skin
and waves of intense pleasure start to spill

across my soul -- my passion now has fed
the empty spot upon my rumpled bed.

Before the Darkness

Before the darkness brings about the night
and steals the world's colors from your sight,
paint all your memories in vivid hues.
Let not the darkness be the path you choose.
Nay! In your dreams, keep every color bright!

You cannot halt the fading of the light,
or still your heart when shadows cause you fright.
So now, decide what defense you will use
before the darkness.

Your darkening fear will offer no respite.
Alas, when all their courage's taken flight,
the strongest men, their battles sometimes lose.
When you most want to hide, you must refuse;
hold firmly in your heart the days delight,
before the darkness.

If Only

I wander this sacred place
among candles and statues,
alone and unseen.

Ephemeral glimpses caught
through thin pastel sheets;
gray tissue-paper smoke.

Time has become only
flowing images, which swirl and eddy
like an oily film on a languid current.

Memories intrude and revolve,
of an onion-skin reality
when breath and temperature mattered.

No escape from these alabaster walls
or from my festering emotions--
of the two, the emotions are worse.

Words like sorrow and regret
are poor substitutions for the anguish,
pain, and guilt--these are all I have left.

if only I had realized
what taking my own life
would really mean...

if only I had listened
to the voices of those
who loved me and now mourn...

if only I didn't know
that forever
is a very real thing...

if only my loneliness
here, where it cannot be ended,
weren't the final enduring remnant...

if only...

The Flame

burn
inside
passion lit
by her shy grin

she shines in the dark
mythic beauty enslaves me
golden dreams of what may be
burned into my soul

a single smile
leads me to
her sweet
fire

Feminine, mysterious - constant changes
I find strange; quite curious,
oh spectral moon, why haunt me thus?

Nighttime sky is your domain - come what may,
day by day, you wax and wane;
your monthly cycle's quite insane.

Like the ocean's ebb and flow - empty, full,
pushing, pulling, to and fro;
so do my lover's passions go.

Moon, you'll stay unknown, I guess - pale and cold,
truth be told, I must confess,
I understand my lover less.

Spectral Moon

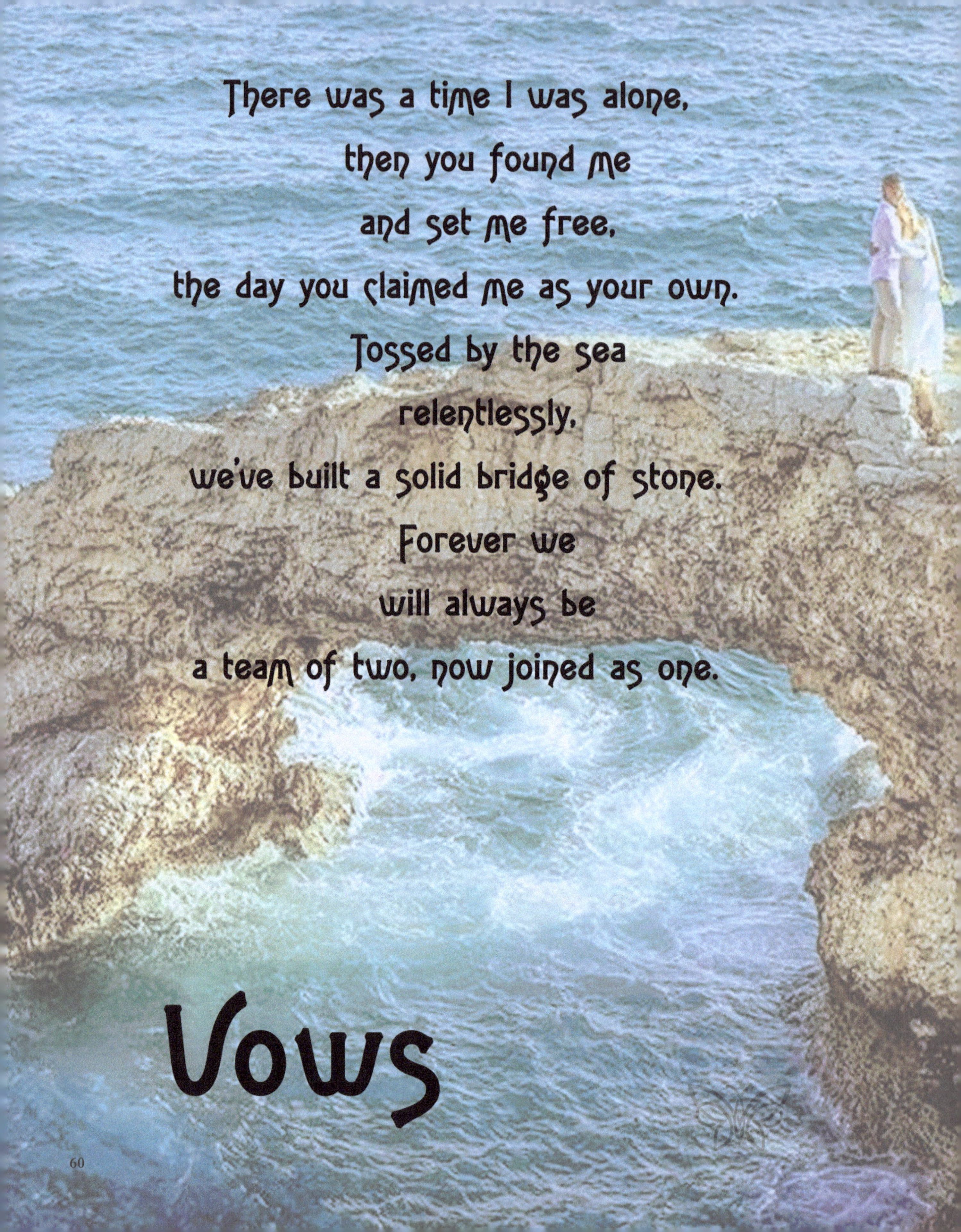

There was a time I was alone,

then you found me

and set me free,

the day you claimed me as your own.

Tossed by the sea

relentlessly,

we've built a solid bridge of stone.

Forever we

will always be

a team of two, now joined as one.

Vows

a mystery

As you can tell   I'm sure we are
　Meant to be in love my dear
　　You tell me to get lost
　　So I leave, but you
　　Turn back to me
　　　Each time I
　　　Run to
　　　You

Ground fog whispers past the trees
and darkness, like my fear, is growing.
Moonlight sparkles in the air, as
through the gloom a subtle glowing
springs to life among the shadows,
outlining my path and showing
clearly on the trail before me,
defying all explanation,
bars of gold, wrought in designs that
fertilize imagination.
From beyond them, a bright clearing
and the sound of celebration,
calling, begging, "Come and tarry,
past the portal
of the Faerie."

The Portal

Standing in the starlit pathway,
wond'ring if I might be dreaming.
Night has fallen left and right; yet
through the gate the sun is streaming!
Music glides upon the breeze and
whispers secrets to me, seeming
maybe too good to be true, and
some deep primal intuition
puts my mind on full alert and
rousing all of my suspicions;
still my feet propel me forward,
almost of their own volition,
my body, they forward carry,
toward the portal
of the Faerie.

Helplessly, I am advancing,
steadily. On legs unfeeling,
o'er the threshold I step swiftly.
Suddenly there comes a healing
of the heart and soul within me,
driving me to my knees. Kneeling,
all the hate and anger falls like
leaves from me, and pure emotion
fills the void. The love I find there,
leads me to pledge my devotion
as the gate dissolves behind me
in a silent light explosion.
Now my past is truly buried,
by the portal
of the Faerie.

My Final Gift

In darkening silence, I followed her footsteps,
impressed in a blanket of snow.
I called out her name and she paused in her flight,
before turning, her dark eyes aglow.

I knew that the pain she now felt was my doing;
each streak down her cheek broke my heart,
yet fate was against us; our young budding romance
was over before it could start.

My family curse had appeared with the full moon;
such hunger could not be denied.
Controlling the beast deep inside was unheard of—
men stronger than I had oft tried.

The hatred for me I saw bloom on her face,
though it hurt, was still better than death;
with eyes full of tears, I then turned, and I whispered
"I love you" soft, under my breath.

She'd go on without me. Though maybe unhappy,
at least I was sure she would live.
Some day I hoped she would find love in her future,
no greater a gift could I give.

Under the Summer Sun

When winter's cold grip is at last undone
and long days give us much more time to play,
what fun we'll have under the summer sun.

    More time we'll have to hop and skip and run
    and spin in circles under sprinkler spray
    when winter's cold grip is at last undone.

    Before we rise, the daylight has begun
    and outside birds have sung the dark away
    what fun we'll have under the summer sun.

    Loud laughter and big smiles for everyone;
    light summer clothes we'll don on cloudless days
    when winter's cold grip is at last undone.

    The smell of grilling grabs our attention
    as picnic goers keep the ants at bay...
    what fun we'll have under the summer sun.

    A campsite near the fire where tales are spun
    next to a lake, far from the crowds we'll stay;
    when winter's cold grip is at last undone,
    what fun we'll have under the summer sun.

Cold and Alone

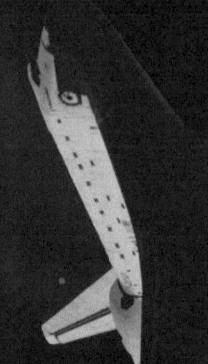

So cold and alone, left to drift silently,
a single light flashing its warning of red
in an icy tin can on an endless black sea,
now piloted only by flash frozen dead.

A small broken window still outlined in lead
and five weightless corpses are testimony
of man's arrogance. A true marvel, they said,
now cold and alone, left to drift silently.

It launched by the numbers. Check one, two and three;
computers on board, streaming data were fed.
On day forty six, the crew looked up to see
one single light flashing its warning of red.

It showed them a meteor shower ahead.
"Evasive maneuvers!" They tried gallantly
but missed a small fragment, which tragically led
to this icy tin can on an endless black sea.

No way to avoid it and nowhere to flee,
in seconds their atmosphere all had been bled.
The craft, now adrift on its trajectory,
is piloted only by flash frozen dead.

The greatest of scientific minds hang their heads.
Exploring the heavens--a dream we set free.
This crowning achievement of science, instead
a tumbling, frozen memorial will be...
ever cold and alone.

Safe and Warm

For forty years and more you've held my hand.
You've seen me fall, and always helped me stand;
there is no danger I'm afraid to face,
when I am safe and warm in your embrace.

You've shared my name, my heart, my life, my bed;
you've shared the dreams I've had within my head.
I've always known, your charm and gentle grace
have kept me safe and warm in your embrace.

We raised our kids, and helped raise their kids too;
been up and down, and back, a time or two.
I've never had to fear losing a race...
they all end safe and warm in your embrace.

We've learned in life, there will be raging storms,
but rainbows, after clouds disperse, will form.
My harbor's always been here just in case,
you need me, safe and warm in your embrace.

In sickness and in health you've stood by me,
together we have built a family.
Regret and doubt, you'll find there's not a trace,
nor sadness, safe and warm in your embrace.

Our time together here now nears its end.
Try not to cry my love, my wife, my friend;
my faith has always had a steady base,
you've held it safe and warm in your embrace.

The light is fading fast—it's time to go.
Never forget, I've always loved you so!
Kiss me. I must your lips one last time taste,
lingering safe and warm in your embrace.

I'll be with you each night inside your dreams;
For Heaven is much closer than it seems.
Hold tight to me as I slip from this place,
forever safe and warm in your embrace.

At the reading of the will the old attorney, he did say
that the property, it needed lots of work and TLC,
but he didn't say the place was truly haunted, night and day,
by the spirit of a woman and a child no one could see.

My Great Grandpa bought the mansion back in Nineteen-Twenty-Three
from a curmudgeon who built it just before the Civil War
for his tender blushing bride, and their intended family,
where together they could forge the future they'd been searching for.

It seemed Fortune smiled brightly on them after they moved in,
when she quickened, and their Happy Ever After had begun;
sadly, joy was but illusion, like a Cheshire kitten's grin,
and in bloody pain he lost them both, his wife and newborn son.

Now abandoned and neglected, since the day it watched them die,
in this house sometimes, a woman singing lullabies is heard
echoed faintly from the shadows by a newborn baby's cry;
yet the lawyer in his wisdom, of this tale spoke not a word.

INHERITANCE

She Lives

She pulled the knife from out her chest.
"Was that supposed to hurt?"
Her evil smile did fear impress,
and panicked thoughts assert.
What evil this, that would not die
from mortal wound? "Alas," said I,
"What evil this?
What evil this,
with heart run though, still does not die?

"Be gone, foul witch!" My echoed scream
did naught but make her grin;
She pulled me close, and whispered "Dream"
The room then seemed to spin.
An icy kiss, softly bestowed
upon my lips, grown deadly cold.
An icy kiss,
an icy kiss
sparked poison fire within my soul.

"Oh foolish man without the will
or faith to stand upon!
You honestly thought you could kill
me, hours before the dawn?"
The darkness calls, I must give in;
for soon my new life will begin.
The darkness calls.
The darkness calls,
and now the hunger grows within.

I woke last night at half-past three
from such a strange nightmare,
of shopping at our local mall
in just my underwear!

Somehow, in this state of undress,
my wife I'd followed there.
She kept insisting it was time
To buy new underwear!

In panic, I searched wildly 'round,
as people stopped and stared.
I looked down, and relieved, I found
I'd worn clean underwear!

Outside the lingerie store now,
a chill rose in the air;
the laughing crowds all pointed at
holes in my underwear!

The thing which brought anxiety,
my wife seemed not to care,
was that there was no dressing room
to change my underwear!

Then worst of all, I felt a slap
upon my derriere;
My wife then winked and leered at me,
Now sans my underwear!

I wakened then, my snoring wife
sleeping without a care,
probably dreaming of shopping,
but not in underwear!

My Nightmare

Death rides on dark wings as the raging storm blows;
the forked lightning patterns echo on the wall.
I cringe and attempt here to hide from my foe
amid the dark ruins of Cumberland Hall.

Harsh thunder rumbles a demonic deep call.
The icy rain soaks me; I've nowhere to go
to hide from the deluge that needle-like falls.
Death rides on dark wings as the raging storm blows.

My heart races faster as time seems to slow;
never have I felt so alone or so small.
My terror is real, on my face it does show;
the forked lightning patterns echo on the wall.

Through crumbling bricks and debris I now crawl
as skeletal fingers of fear start to grow.
Pure fright wraps around me, a poisonous shawl;
I cringe and attempt here to hide from my foe.

Tempestuous gusts seek to find me below
the ebony storm cloud's encompassing pall.
Cold eddies of wind whip wet leaves, to and fro,
amid the dark ruins of Cumberland Hall.

Defiant, I rise up and try to stand tall.
A lightning bolt answers, as if to say "No!"
Falling back down, I curl into a ball;
a fluttering reaches my ears and I know.
Death rides on dark wings.

Death Rides on Dark Wings

Beware the wood, where shadows black as night
cavort like living dark between the trees,
for thus has entered many a glorious knight,
high-riding, strong and brave, upon a steed...
    now naught but gallant memories remain.
    Here many ancient secrets are retained
    and those who seek to make this place their own
    must have no sins for which they need atone.
        'Tis said that human souls find demon-sleep,
        and every one is lost, whose lot is thrown
        among the trees within the forest deep.

    Slow fog creeps in, and quickly fades the light;
    salvation has become a primal need,
    while shadows twist, encouraging your fright
    and glowing eyes betray some evil breed.
        Dark clouds do cast upon the moon a stain
        which dims faint lunar light towards black again.
        A raspy voice, as of some ageless crone,
        calls out your name and chills you to the bone.
            As inky shadows round your body creep,
            prepare your soul to face threats yet unknown
            among the trees within the forest deep.

        O foolish man, it does no good to fight
        against an enemy who does not bleed!
        A lightning flash just at the edge of sight
        frightens your horse, now struggling to break free.
            It rolls its eyes and screams in mortal pain
            as twisting branches grasp, and then restrain.
            On stiffened knees it gives one final groan,
            and topples to the earth, its body stone.
                Now must you venture onward as you weep,
                for unseen creatures howl and loudly moan,
                among the trees within the forest deep.

Too late now to avoid your wretched plight,
your fear swells deep inside, a vile weed.
Dank moss, and fungus yellowing with blight,
soon plant within your soul an evil seed;
   then, when it seems you must go quite insane,
   a voice behind you says, "Let me explain."
You draw your sword and spin, your fear full blown,
but no one's there; you are still quite alone.
      The rending of the dark makes your heart leap,
      you find blue-tinged witchfire has quickly grown
      among the trees within the forest deep.

Feet frozen fast, unable to take flight,
you're paralyzed by some unholy deed
and evil Fae folk, foul eyes shining bright,
grin as they dine; on rancid flesh they feed,
   and sup on drink brewed from some bitter grain.
   Your sanity, you're desperate to retain
as courage, like chaff, to the wind is thrown
upon their devil's pile of gristled bones.
      In horror you see, o'er the putrid heap,
      a wrinkled Elven Queen upon a throne,
      among the trees within the forest deep.

Based on the witch's smile, your fate is known;
One evil kiss, and all free will has flown.
Your cursed soul's no longer yours to keep--
damnation, from within her eyes has shone
      among the trees within the forest deep.

Within The Forest Deep

Fading memories blow
through my dry empty soul,
wrapped in echoes of
    tormented silence and pain
like a hot desert wind,
past the crumbling facade
of a ghost town, abandoned,
    where tumbleweeds reign.

Like emotional stretch marks
carved into my heart,
inky shadows lie twisted
    and deeply embossed
in striations and patterns
that spell out your name
etched in acid-rain tears,
    spilled for all that I've lost.

When I let myself ponder
the cruelty of fate,
the unfairness still twists
    in my guts like a knife.
Since you left me behind
without saying goodbye,
deep blue loneliness colors
    the rest of my life.

In my dreams you're still here
    and still sharing my bed,
then I wake all alone,
    with your voice in my head.

A Lonely Appendix

Alas, my loves, I think I soon must go,
As dusk has fallen, and my time's at hand.
Ah, children, there's one lesson you should know
Aging, and time, have made me understand.
All of the negatives we've ever felt,
Any hurts that we've buried and denied;
Anger about the bad hands we were dealt
And wretched bitterness we've tried to hide,
Are washed away, like sand against the tide.

At The End

As grief and pain, like sand against the tide,
Are washed away, our hearts are free again
And we can choose just what to let inside
After deciding to let go of pain.
Against the love that's left, nothing can win,
All of the world's problems amount to naught
Any of you can choose now to begin
Applying all the lessons love has taught,
And storing deep the joys that can't be bought.

Always embrace the joys that can't be bought
Assist a friend in need without a care,
And render aide without a second thought.
Ask after those with whom you can't be there,
Avoid leaving unsaid the words of praise,
And make sure those you do love, always know,
As no one knows the number of their days.
Ah! Gather close and kiss me, eyes aglow,
Alas my loves, it's time for me to go.

About the Poet

Dusty Grein is an Accredited Classical Poet whose work has appeared in journals, books, magazines, and online publications. His best-selling, critically heralded novel The Sleeping Giant introduced readers to his distinctive blend of narrative depth and imaginative storytelling.

A Mist Shrouded Path is his first full collection of poetry. Drawing from both traditional and contemporary forms, Dusty weaves stories through meter, imagery, and emotional resonance, creating work that speaks to readers of all ages.

He makes his home in the forests and mountains of the Pacific Northwest. When not writing or exploring new creative pursuits under his Flitterbow Productions banner, he enjoys exercising his mind and wandering the quiet corners of the internet.

Published by
Flitterbow Productions

© 2018, 2025 All Rights Reserved